SKY

JAMIE MCKENDRICK
Sky Nails

Poems 1979–1997

faber and faber

LONDON·NEW YORK

First published in 2000
by Faber and Faber Limited
3 Queen Square London WC1N 3AU
Published in the United States by Faber and Faber, Inc.,
a division of Farrar, Straus and Giroux, Inc., New York

Photoset by Wilmaset Ltd, Wirral
Printed in England by
MPG Books Limited, Victoria Square, Bodmin, Cornwall

Jamie McKendrick is hereby identified as author
of this work in accordance with Section 77
of the Copyright, Designs and Patents Act 1988

A CIP record for this book
is available from the British Library

ISBN 0–571–20178–4

2 4 6 8 10 9 7 5 3 1

For Posy and Michael O'Neill

Contents

from THE MARBLE FLY (1997)

Ill Wind

To talk of the weather was a morbid sign.
The winds blew wherever they wanted to
raining their freight of dust.
A week before, the sirocco had come
with its tiny pouches of sand, transplanting
one grain at a time the whole Sahara;
silting the windows with a fine tan.
But this was a wind from the north that blew
across frontiers, ignoring the Customs.
If it blew somewhere else the papers were glad.

I brushed a spider from the web it'd spun
between my arm and what seemed to be air –
it fell by a thread then hobbled off,
its fifth or its sixth leg giving it trouble.
'Will they survive it all,' you asked, 'the insects?'
I remembered the mutation-rates we'd studied
of the fruit fly (short-, long- and cross-winged)
and a luminous dream I'd had of origin:
life spiralling out from the cradled cell
through the basking oceanic forms.

And though the leaves were still I heard the wind
snicking the links with its casual shears.

Frail Weave

By ions or ozone or iodine,
light unimpaired from the horizon –
how the sea signals itself
by an inkling long before
the hightide crashes on the ear and pines
end in plants splayed and hackled
by the seawind is a mystery
as though a sea inside were answering exactly
with its own miniature lapsing crests
wearing away at an interior shore:
sometimes just inches sometimes whole towns
spirited away in the undertow.

*

Its pebble-chafing, bone-comb undertow.
The old edge of Suffolk lies under the sea;
Dunwich capsized from the Commonwealth
keeps its afterlife of hotels, craftshops,
a harmless wry affair, while down the coast
the squat domain of Sizewell
voids its heat through a pipe into the sea.

*

Sea-anglers dot the foreshore, their rods
like the jittery feelers of crayfish
or the dials of a Geiger counter.
But now the whole heath spreads
violet, salt-kissed, tightly curled
on its bed of peat where the ling and the bell
and the cross-leaved heather cling

in dusky mounds to the earth that holds
on an edge, the dearer for its vanishing.

*

By the sea's edge I coveted the mermaid's purse
(egg-case of the common skate) and the sea-pecked
interior shell of the cuttlefish shaped
like a balsawood pelvis – its ghostly bulk
steered through crizzled veils of ink. The low cliffs
are fraying, leaving packed layers of peat
studded with egg-pale stones exposed
like a wall whose verge is
held by the frailest weave of marram grass.

Living in Sin

We were never at home in that house, the home
of the Bishop of Truro's widow:
our personalities were too small, our words
seemed to tail off and to touch
was a day's journey across the flowered divan.
When friends came to stay we put on
a brave face, took meals off the oak table
and walked around as if we owned the place.

Even our books were outnumbered and outflanked
by their leatherbound tomes. I felt evil
as a water-spider in an air-bubble
leafing through the annotated Bible
yet I began to understand his recreations
– mainly Daniel and Revelations.
The seven hills of Babylon meant Rome
and, once there, he went to town on scarlet
and fornication, lulling himself with wrath.
666 would ring a bell at
the Pope's bedside or was it upside-down,
I wondered, implicating the police?

Much of it was illegible, but that spiky hand
reached out of the grave with its NBs
and admonitory rapping commentaries
as the Victorian engravings on the stairs
we wanted to, but never dared, remove
had bodies in chaste nightgowns rising from
a host of cracked-asunder sepulchres
lock-jawed, stiff-jointed and justified.

We were thieves that had stolen into the fold
waiting to be discovered and expelled
by a flaming sword. The widow's letter came
more terrible than flames, more tearful
at what I don't think we had meant to hide
– 'our situation'. It was clear she saw
the Unclean coupling in the Inner Sanctum,
brazen and tireless and 'under her roof'.
If only what we'd done had given proof
to her acrobatic fantasy, if only
the empty rooms had echoed with our cries
we might have felt less wronged. At the year's end

we were given notice and her middle-aged son,
squinting at us with unspeakable pleasure,
said he was sorry but they'd decided
to sell. He helped me shift the tea-chests
and his eyes fell on your clothes as though dazed
in a perfumed garden. Two weeks later
a young married couple were the new tenants
filling the house, making themselves at home.

&

A born rebel, at ease in your outrage
you refuse the armchair's invitation
to slump in a heap or sleep in a hump.

I'm by contrast on a hardbacked chair
sitting prim and tightarsed as Britannia
with a shield of books and a chewed biro.

The argument we're having is unravelling
the ends that look so odd now
they're asunder, we can only wonder

how they ever did get joined together.
It seems we've unwound an ampersand and
pulled it like a cracker. On the third chair

the black-and-white cat and the white-and-black,
love-locked in a tricky double helix,
keep licking each other's necks.

Fetish

That my first car, at thirty, should be fifth-hand,
a filthy patchwork of worn azure and bare zinc
and amateur spray-jobs like a subway wall,

appeals to my pride as a failed consumer.
Its faults I can cherish as if they were my own.
What does it matter that its lights are dimmer,

that each year a psoriasis of rust is rising
from its mudguards and its bodywork has travelled
countless kilometres from the original plan

when something inside miraculously
keeps going, going against the predictions
of its detractors – who are vile, and legion.

What does it matter it's not long for this world
when shards of it, its polished tyres for instance,
are primed to outlast the most resistant

and cared-for of my bodily remains.
There is so much to thank it for. It makes
my superfluous entrances and exits

possible, that would have been difficult
or undreamt-of, otherwise. It gives me
the illusion of progress and takes away thought

like television, replacing it with a system of mirrors,
reflexes and recognitions like a Kertész photo.
It takes me places that I thought I'd never see

even though seeing them is not that different
from not having seen them – but who's to say
if experience doesn't help, doing nothing does?

[7]

It teaches me a deep metallic pillow-talk
of mounting lugs drive shafts seal lips and bleeder valves
and, in the stale inches of the traffic jam,

lip-reading, hand gestures and slow footwork.
It provides a haven to smoke and talk in
when there's rain, a host to our interminable

arguments, a roadside seat, a mobile cupboard,
a crystal kiosk and a rubbish dump
– civilization emptied of its discontents.

Cornbride

The cornfield
is a gold comb
or a sunned fleece
the wind grooms

to a shadow
or perhaps a cloud
the wind kites
is trailing shadow

miles behind
as a bride trails
broad muslin veils
in daylight outside

though already
she's being led
with a light tread
along the aisle.

Rite de Passage

The foreign place-names sped past like blurred print —
solemn, unpronounceable inscriptions —
as she sat with the terracotta jar
between her knees and spelt out the sign
on the steel tag screwed to the window-frame:
NE JETEZ AUCUN OBJET PAR LA FENÊTRE.
Her knuckles whitened round the neck of the jar.
Some corner of a foreign field ... he never
gave a toss for that. He'd sold his medals
for coppers under the sign of the three brass balls
and come out beaming – a weight off his chest –
but the first time back since the last war,
his first 'jaunt' abroad to stop like a clock
not to cough wake up wink not to nod or grin
not to anything anymore – that was more than bad luck;
it was everything weightless and insipid
like mothwings crushed in linen or love-letters burned
to a talcy wad. She expected something
more cumbersome to fetch back. At Dover,
where the gulls fought and the passengers filed
toward Customs, she didn't join the queue
and her granddaughter, guarding the suitcase,
watched her walk back slowly to the quay,
stand, unbalanced, peering from the edge
then pour him out like an offering to the birds.
He rested a while on the oil-film
faintly and a little aloof, a grey smudge
fading and darkening into the waters.

from Lost Cities

A Lost City

Heaven is the country of the exiles.
They travelled here for refuge or for rest,
To learn the language or to taste the fruit.
Years pass. A cloud occludes the mountain's foot
And the road home is overgrown with mist,
The white edges of a virgin forest
Neither daytrip nor exodus defiles.

The bread is good and bitter but still leaves
The palate aching for an absent flavour.
The shopping malls have windows where you find
Instead of your own face, a heedful neighbour
Whose joy to find you may be just as feigned.
Is your face too, so transfigured and tanned?
Less old each day, less coarsened by beliefs?

Perhaps this isn't heaven after all.
The walls are veined with rose and polished beryl
– An ichor that you don't know how to tap.
New arrivals are treated with such awe,
Robed in colours, in light, as if each step
They take will help us trace some lost Before
Which if it ever was we can't recall.

Another Lost City

The frock-coated twins, with their boxer's shoulders,
Have parked their hearse outside the jewellers.
I steel myself to look them in the eyes.
Behind smoked glass, their three dark brides are swathed
In ivory satin. If only they'd escape!
The sea clops and blisters like boiling clay.
On the quayside the guards have laid a table
And lean to feed the new guests shark-meat
From pitchforks. Others stroll along the seafront
On living stones the mottled colour of skin.
The sounds they make are not the same as words.
But you can't complain when the air they breathe
Is molten glass and the guidebook has
No sooner opened than burst into flame.

Decadence

It was the time of day when the soul speaks Latin
with a Gothic slur, and sees in every direction
an evening made of basil and magenta.

There was no breeze, and we were walking
by the canals and office-blocks of Carthage.
You were in a sour mood and foresaw

only war and burning, widows and orphans.
I suggested we stop at a bar for sherbet
– the latest thing, sprinkled with ginger.

From there, we could see the queen on her terrace
sporting her would-be wedding gown, its train
of damask roses twined with ears of corn.

The light took on a green tinge and a drunk
ex-mercenary kept muttering about drift-lines
where banded kraits would coil to clean their scales

– diamonds glittering in the sea-junk.
It made no sense to me, but sense
was not what I was after. I wanted dreams.

As dusk drew in its final flecks of gold
I felt the black north couching in my bones.

Margin

Some played volleyball using fishing nets;
some drank cans of Peroni; others searched
inland for flints and sources of clear water.

I wandered by the shore towards the harbour
and the blind lighthouse of Palinurus,
and found a dolphin turning at the tide's hem

bluntly, its skin fraying on the sharp stones;
then the stringy, knifed wheeze of the helmsman
came back from the shadows and a light struck

fire through the mute larynx of the rock
at Cumae – the mad woman humming just to calm him:
That cruel place will always bear your name.

Nostalgia

I woke drenched in sweat and homesick
for nowhere I could think of, a feeling
scuffed and quaint as farthings or furlongs.

Then I remembered the room of the sirocco
in a Sicilian palace made of pink volcanic sugar.
There was a scent of waxed oak and pistachios.

Two maids were making up our nuptial bed,
smoothing the white linen with their dark hands.
You'd never have finished finding fault in their work

if I hadn't intervened, so that you turned on me
saying *Their family were turnip doctors
at the time of the Bourbons* – an old enmity then,

and more imperious even than pleasure.
How to get out of that windowless room,
with not one of its walls adjoining the air

was all I could think of, from that point on.
Your voice pursued me down the marble stairway:
Don't think you'll ever find a home again!

Memory

The staff are picketing the pleasure gardens
of the Baia Hotel with placards.
The sun is trying to melt the rocks.

The Hohenzollerns and the Hohenstaufens
are having their annual conference inside
while their saffron-tinted, air-conditioned coaches

loaf in the parking lot above the cliff
and their drivers try to read the placards
– something about the bay being soiled,

a filter, and embezzled public funds.
I've got to know each curve of this coast road
as the car hairpins like a cardiograph.

(From a distance, it is gently bow-shaped.)
I know where a barn-owl nests and where
the agaves leap from their rootstock toeholds

and could tell of the netted lemon groves
that hesitate on parapets so narrow
you want to talk them back to safety;

and of the watchtowers underwater,
the window where a moray eel is curled ...
but I won't – this need to depict

is just a weakening of the hold I have
on that rockface, a fatal stepping-backwards
onto glazed blue tiles that are tiles of air.

Axle-Tree

I lurk like a stowaway in the dark threshold
of your block of flats and wait for a sign.

I park my wreck beside the lorries that slouch
at the curb till dawn, laden to the tusks
with mahogany logs from Senegal.

At the docks, just a caber's toss away,
where row after row of raw pink Fiats
are waiting for Legion to possess them,

they season in heaps and no sooner move
than they come to a halt, as if obeying
some natural imperative. Your balcony

gives on timber seeping resin
in the moonlight; the mountains bracketing
the bay's black waves as they fret

the sea-front and the frail hull
of the unfrequented *Nave-Ristorante*
moored under the cement factory's toxic plume.

It's all crammed in like a tourist's map.
Nightshifts, headlamps and the desultory tide.
The palm fronds shrugging on the promenade.

Loosed from the shaggy leggings of those logs
I expect a windfall of treesnakes and insects
to seep through the holes of my peel-back roof.

Only last week a scorpion stung you.
Starting as a fire on the side of your thigh
it came to a head in a charred violet point...

You became irascible and superstitious
and dreamed of a horrible martyrdom.
You felt my star-sign made me somehow to blame.

as if I'd hired a familiar for the crime.
My car fell under suspicion. You began to call it
The Touring Insect House, checking the seats

and shadows on entering, where before
you'd merely likened it to the bin-skips
with their beds of decomposing ash-blue mulch.

I've my doubts too. Do lovers use it by night?
Its suspension is not what it used to be.
Beer bottles, cigarette packets with odd

brand-names, chewed gum-wads: all add up to something
– nocturnal depredations! Anything could live there
biodegrading, unobserved, while the rear-mirror

makes headlights flare like stars snapped out of fixity
and the hewn trunks seem lengths of a broken axle
around which once the leaf-green planet turned.

De-signifiers

Rust and dry rot and the small-jawed moth
are our best friends and they wish us well,
undoing the fabric of our heaven.

They correspond to something inside us
that doesn't love the works our hands have made
– wire-cutters, pick-locks, saboteurs.

'Are you building a good memory to have of me?'
you once asked as though I'd just begun
a papier-mâché Taj Mahal.

I keep a cardboard box of newspapers
in the cupboard so everything that's happened
is safe from pulp mills and the record-shredders

but all the while in the dark the silverfish
and woodlice are at work on the word,
its dot matrix. Living on what seems to us

dust, they profit directly from our negligence
and attention in general only provokes
their swerving, averting or curling-up manoeuvres.

Meaning? They roll it away and break it down
into unrecombinable fragments
like fatigue in our metal or cancer in concrete.

Il Capitano

He keeps a dark shed by the beach-huts and boat-houses
smelling of diesel and damp wool;
there's a yellowed notice tacked to the door
in a strange hand, or a strange tongue like the babble
of waves on pebbles, cursives of broken shell.

Bound in his nets and tackle, he carries a trident
to tap the ground in the tireless pacing
that keeps him always in sight of the sea
where the spiny rocks sift back the waves
like krill-less drizzle from the teeth of whales.

The villagers tell how once, years back,
he commanded a vessel wrecked miles out
and drifted days on a fragment of deck.
Ever since his rescue he's lived like the last man alive
in this coast resort buzzing with tourists and Vespas.

He was washed up here like the rest of us
by seed, tide, trade or fate but clearly lives,
oblivious of custom, under a different sky
– the stars urgent and legible; the miles of black salt
crashing into coves, his intimate blueprint.

It's said that sometimes he sights a ship
far out in the blue and foams with an exquisite
panic of recognition. Dropping his stick
he thrashes through the waves like a fierce child
till the fishermen gently drag him back again.

Sign Language

The deaf-mute fisherman sits in his beached boat
with the net he's mending looped round both big toes
and his left-hand thumb while his right hand weaves
in and out. Air and water crash in soundless waves
through the spaces where his livelihood will catch,
the fishes whose new names I'm slowly learning:
merluzzo, alice, dentice, pesce spada . . .
Seeing me reading, he signs that books are better
– what he earns in a day I spend in an hour
eating fish at the restaurant he supplies.

Motorini swarm in from the cities
of the plain, from the little badlands
under the shadow of Vesuvius. Then when the bars
are closed, the cars in the car park rock like boats,
their windows taped with *Il Mattino* or *L'Unità*
and I see him picking his way home
through the refuse of a beach-culture
with nothing but a bemused welcoming smile
– though when he stops outside his door I'd swear
he's talking to himself with his fluent hands.

Darkness in the Mezzogiorno

Rubbish clots the courtyard's fountain sculpture
of Neptune clouting a triton with a fishbone.
There's a smell of rotting cuttlefish
off the cobbles, and an iridescent sludge
of rosy scales and silver fishes' eyes. The sea
is everywhere, and nowhere visible, like God.
It sweats through the walls where sand from the sea
was used four centuries ago for stucco.
These alleys where the local kings and *pezzi grossi*
hung out from verdant balconies
are still rich as any royal family
in the underwater categories of crime,
and seethe with bullet-headed shoals
of *ruffiani*, *spacciatori*, *camorristi*.
In winter the prostitutes sit warming
their slack calves over a fire of fruit crates.
A lack of expectation lights
along the false blonde's unbruised olive eyes.
Everything that happens happens on the streets
or overlooking them. There's no elbow-room
under the sign AREA DI MANOVRA:
for the old men playing *scopa* where
the pavement ought to be; for cars
that back up the way they came or
airwaves jammed with radios and rows;
no room to retreat where history
has made a fig-sign at the private life.
Lost empires jostle in the cellarage
and layer after layer of colonists lie shelved
under the cobbles with their dialects
and utensils – Roman, Saracen and Spaniard –

their rubbish and their triumphs petrified:
jewel-hilted daggers and medical tracts
rhymed in Latin; lacquered fans and vessels carved
for Christendom by Arab ebonists...
Down there are knots that no one can undo,
wounds fingerprints and pomegranate seeds,
bedheads and olivestones and shoulderblades
in sheets of salt hid from the light of day.

Mermaid

My mistake was not to leave a breathing space,
a vacuole for firing in the kiln
but I was only thinking of the shape
she'd grow into, sleek and seal-grey, her flanks
basted with a patina of sea-slime.
She didn't look like something that could last,
washed-up, drying from the outside inwards,
a shade more pallid every day, but the limbs
I was lucky with – the arch of the back,
the balance of her small provocative head
and the breasts on which I'd lavished
more than a cameo-maker's care. The tail
was cleftless, with the usual scales
etched by a pin. So how did mermaids mate?
No doubt they found some way, agonizingly
metamorphic, for their cast-ashore princes
though I strayed no nearer a solution
than the faintest hint. On that coastal windowsill
she sat battening on the muzzled crash the waves
made on the rocks, draining in tiny rills.

When she broke she broke across the navel
in a break so fine she could still balance
without glue on those stunning ichthyian hips.
The second crack came in an argument
at the curve where her knees would have been.
There was a storm and the sea crashed against the mole.
Then, when we moved to make way for the rich
summer tenants, among boxes of stones and shells,
the beachcombed chips off seaworn tiles
she took more punishment – her nose crumbled

and her face became the fate of Cresseid
in the drypoint version of Henryson.
She stayed among discarded things
stacked in the back of my battered Citroën,
its scalloped bonnet like the boat of Venus,
until the day the sea-storm peeled the roofs
from the beach-huts and a great wave palled
the piazza with saltwater, waistdeep
where the cars were parked ... there, in the boot,
I found a layer of sand and nothing more
than a grey trace, a silt of potter's clay.

Under the Volcano

Between the Devil's Viaduct and the deep blue sea,
any darkened patch or nook will do,
they gather for the rites of youth
– a soluble nectar that arrives
from nowhere, like a boat in the port.

Incendi dolosi. A bronze light worries
the night sky where the hillside
consumes itself. Those
wanting compensation tie
a burning brand to a trapped bird's foot

so where the bird alights in terror
flames spread. No one's
the wiser as when the camorra
firebomb a discotheque or bar.
You sense the sulphur under the earth's crust

The cortège follows the boy
they found in the Park of Springtime,
his forearm dandling a syringe.
Between the viaduct and the seafront
you crush the brittle flowers underfoot.

Incendi dolosi: arson

The Vulcanologist

Athanasius   Kircher
having   completed   his
key work on Coptic grammar
(and   rightly   linked   it   to   the
hieroglyphs)   left   the   cardinals
in Rome and set about his Latin tract
on volcanoes. He visited Etna and Vesuvius,
and Vesuvius he entered, let down the inner
walls by lengths of rope, growing smaller and
smaller like a bug on a thread tacked to the sky's
vault with tiny pins of adamant. There he swung past
fumaroles with poison yellow plumes, abseiling through
gardens of brimstone and red cinders. He saw the vestibule
he knew would lead to a vast network of subterranean flames,
lakes of bitumen and burning conduits threading land and ocean
from Iceland to Patagonia. In his book he mapped fire's empire and
its outposts, the whole racked body of Hephaestos, whose molten hea
we build our spindly cities on, and plant and tend our perishable gro

The Earth's Rind
after Eugenio Montale

The Earth's rind is finer, more close-grained
than an apple's skin – if we assume
the material world is not
just an illusion. Nonetheless
we're stuck in this nothing, if such
we admit it is, up to our necks.
The pessimists say that what sticks
us here is everything we've made
to replace the gods. But the old God's
still faithful followers assert
this substitution didn't take.
Perhaps He'll come, they say, in person
to prize us from the magma limb
by limb. So we live and are
a double life, even if the self-
adoring would choose only one.
O mother Earth, O Heaven
of celestial beings – it's this
that's the problem,
that makes us mad and shriller than
a bird in lime.

Ye Who Enter In
after Antonio Machado

To plumb the depths of hell and meet
ministers, saladins and scholars,
Marilyn Monroe and Cleopatra,
the latter naked as the day they died;
to give audience where you please
and where you don't to curl your lip
or deftly rabbit-punch a kidney,
sure that your arm is power-assisted.
To be steered about by someone who just
happens to be Virgil, and you like his poems.
To write as a chisel writes on rock
so every phrase you write resounds forever:
ABANDON ALL HOPE ... You first.
No really I insist please after you.

Back from the Brink

like the time I went to sleep while driving
and began to dream that there was something
wrong with the car – the noise it made
was ominous like liquid looking

for a hairline crack, some brittle chink
it meant to rip wide open or explode
so I drove it in my dream to the mechanic's
– a shoggly booth he'd roofed with zinc –

where he looked it over, shook his head
and told me that the problem was electric
though luckily his friend across the road
(and here I must have steered across the road)

would fix it. But his friend said what I'd need
was a real maestro in hydraulics
– and one with wings at least if, hearing Greek,
I hadn't slammed my foot down on the brake.

Sky Nails

That first day, to break me in,
my hardened comrades
sent me scampering like a marmoset
from the topmost parapet

to the foreman's hut
for a bag of sky nails.
The foreman wondered which precise
shade of blue I had in mind.

It's still sky nails I need today
with their faint threads
and unbreakable heads

that will nail anything
to nothing
and make it stay.

The Seismographical Survey

Crumbling the tarmac into treacly clods
tufts of weed were using their green levers
on the disused airfield we drove across
to load our jeep up from the magazine
– that padlocked booth among the bulrushes
stacked with boxes of waxed cardboard sticks
and fuses trailing nervous wires . . .
We'd start where yesterday's fresh boreholes
lipped with screws of clay
made ten-yard strides across Derbyshire
then stop beside each hole and blow it up.
I tamped the 1 lb. stick of dynamite
with a nine-foot copper-ended pole
and fixed the fuse-wires to the detonator
which Arthur plunged so that the thump and spray
would surface as a heartbeat on the graph
in the technician's van which followed us
dark-windowed, white, a kind of ambulance.
And casualties occurred
though they were after something under us;
I never found out whether coal or oil
but Arthur's guess was that they found fuck all.
Day after day we'd trample through and cancel
field after field of corn rape barley pasture
and the odd head-high field of sunflowers
and in our wake we sowed a line of craters
and echoes beaking down through soil and bedrock
and sods and divots falling in slow-motion.

The last day we bumped into this farmer
sleepily trudging through a field of his

balancing two offcuts of one coathanger
bent into right-angles.
After we'd shed our loaded shoulderbags
he showed us how to hold those L-shaped wires
lightly, how they made an X
above the water-channels we took on trust
then gradually uncrossed as we walked on
and how this other way with our own hands
we answered to those echoes underground.

Et In Orcadia Ego

Having heard the Orkneys were like Eden
we sold up everything and bought a farm.
A subsistence farm, I called it. There wasn't sun
enough for solar panels – the rays fell
at such an oblique angle, it was clear
they were heading for somewhere else,
some kinder place with trees. All round the year
the big winds tore about with wasteful power.
I felt that just by being there
I was tilting at windmills. Did I have to
build them as well? Since then I've often thought
if we'd run the water-pipes beneath the henshit
like smoky lava on the floor of the coop
we could have had hot water winterlong.

The last straw was a goat-breeding project.
Hoping the meat might sell, I'd bought
this Anglo-Nubian billy to beget
a nation and populate our land. I left him
tethered to a mulberry shrub ... when God
stumbled upon the body of Abel
in the murderous quiet of the day
and sent Cain off to chew the bitter cud
he must have felt as I felt in that empty place.
The farm pony was looking darkly innocent
and the kid had withdrawn into his yellow gaze
– the colour made me think of Nile mud –
his jaw stove in by the pony's hoof.
All attempts to heal or tend him failed
and, though neither I nor Anne could keep it down,
we ended eating our last chance to stay.

The Wrong Side

They fled the village when the mountainside
loosed a hail of boulders through their roofs. I stayed
in the one house left standing, a guest house
in a ghost town of cracked jambs and gaping doorways.
The man I shared with was unfortunately mad.
Rage and soft-spokenness, the poles he swung between,
were inseparable as the two chained sticks
he whirled about his head for martial exercise.
The generator at the back hummed like an iron locust
that would take off one day and turn the sky black.

Too good to be true (neither her strong point)
she arrived one morning but was followed.
Goats chewed the shadows of the rock and gazed
with proprietorial sarcasm
and planted themselves in my path to watch me
hesitate. On either side the vipers generated:
slack, small, untied like black boot laces,
their heads just big enough to hold one thought . . .

The kitchen had a noble view
of the circle of mountains that hemmed us in,
the air tasselled with heat and a viaduct
exerting itself above a riverbed
now dusty as a crater or a grate.
Straight down from that window was a sheer drop
into an elderberry wilderness – just one wrong foot,
a footfall, a rockfall, a word at the earth's core
would have had us head over heels in roots
and treetops, crashing through a valley of shadows.

The shadow of her breasts was nard and henna,
her lap a garden of elderberries
but my time was up and a car came for her.
Each day I walked to the new village where the old village
had regrouped, with its one-eyed bar and square
in the middle of which was a palm tree up to its chin
in white dust. I watched a chained goat on the slope
trying, without finesse, to befriend a hen
and coping with rejection time and again.
Then there was the station where some trains would stop

for practice I supposed. Or to catch their breath.
The lines led off to somewhere I'd begun
long before to lose faith in. By the blind ticket booth
a sign spoke four languages. The English read:
IT IS FORBIDDEN TO CROSS THE TOACKS.
That summer I came to know the Toacks
– with their roots hooked under the earth's crust.
On the right side of them you'd never guess
they even existed but from where I was
they were too deep to fathom and too tall to cross.

The Agave

also called aloe, maguey, the century plant,
only seems to flourish where
an inch would launch it into space

on cliffs and ledges and descents
beside the prickly pears that crouch
in their hairsuits like luscious grudges.

Saw-toothed, sword-shaped, its fleshy leaves
are carved with hearts and hard-ons
by agile Orlandos.

After twenty, sometimes thirty years,
out of the powerhouse of its rootstock
from which the Aztecs brewed

their pulque and clear-eyed mescal,
it sprouts a lone stem limbed with bright
unbelliferous panicles

twenty, sometimes thirty foot tall
and at a rakish angle to the rock
then dies to leave the coastline

studded with the charred masts
and gutted decks of an armada.

Loss

If what you hear is like a field
and the height of a lark above it
then the field has dwindled and the wind
bells on the razor wire around
the verge beyond which nothing
but the pointless din of outer space,
the addled Muzak of the spheres,
gets through to you. Acoustic junk.
The earth itself begins to hum
with the infinitesimal tunnelling
of umpteen holts and vaults and brood halls
and the sky each dawn is lower than
the day before as though wound down
like a press-head on a worm-screw
where once you woke and heard the threads
of birdsong trailed from hedge to hedge
as clear and intricately round
as a palm-bark epic in Telugu.

Tinnitus

The rustle of foil, a tide of pins, a wave
which never breaking
crinkles from the far side of the brink

and inches nearer with its crest
of decibels and wreckage under which
still you catch the cars diminishing, phrase

after phrase of the evening bird
fainter each time but holding out
from a twig upon a tree within a wood.

Terminus

Io ero tra color che son sospesi

Hanging on the hours like heliotropes
we have taken root where we set foot;
the sun favours our recreations
and salt in the seawind glazes us over
with a tan, a patina, taken for health.

We greet each other with averted eyes
and shipwrecked smiles. Otherwise
indulge in the stern vice of vivisection
and self-portraiture: exiles who left
for no reason with no reason to return.

The Crystal Sky

The city of glass was throwing stones
of glass at the neighbouring city of stone.
Then nothing happened worth reporting.

I lived in an outcrop cube of thinnest glass,
a little showcase of bad habits
– unspeakable things I did at night

waiting for the Reprisal, the moon aqueous
rose-coloured, almost within reach.
The person I like to think of as my friend

suffered my late calls detecting
an illness too limpid for the textbooks.
A glass tide tinkled on the hull

of the receiver, its echoing obsidian.
Our voices rocked on the pauses, becalmed.
That pipette of plantfood had made the agave

sprout two feet in one day – it was too much
the way it swigged litres of fresh water
as if survival was so important.

Between the moon and my see-through roof
a purple storm was blowing the dust
of some previous war into the waste spaces.

Then in the brittle hour before dawn
it occurred to me there might might there not
still be time to set my house in order.

Windrose

When we threw caution to the winds, the city
was the city of winds which blew from the eight points,
   the four quarters
of the windrose, a star which creaked and skittered on its hinge
and reared dustdevils – helices, rootless, footloose, almost human –

and a palm frond swept the public garden paths
like a bird feigning lameness – shuffle, hop, another shuffle –
while a plinth of sunlight turned the sea's roof turquoise
and tides lashed the concrete calthrops of the breakwater.

On a calm day once from Posillipo I saw
the sea, way out, extrude a pillar of salt, a corkscrew
that tapped the deep and lifted shoals to rain down on our roofs
like wingless birds who'd flown through sheer assumption.

Mountain

Ledge

The mountain would have crashed on top of us
but it needed to unlace its concrete stays
and the wire mesh that caged its overhang.

Lilies splashed with fire from the underworld
grew in a niche beneath the barn-owl's nest
– all night we heard her catastrophic wheezing

and the even breathing of the tideless sea
down where the steps expired, tired of counting,
of footsoles, heels, of having to be steps

so far below while up above as far
the coast road curled and shed its cast-offs
for the morning on the balcony:

a ripe fig, a hairclip, a fag-end, a feather
and a faint premonitory sprinkling of stones.

On the Volcano

For years in the shadow of the mountain
we'd never thought to cast our shadows on it,
to peep down into it from up above...

Slag and clinkers; an afterthought that still
plagues the earth about her final form;
a verruca; a welt; a peak of hell

erected in the midst of paradise.
Fumes idled up the inner walls
as we stopped at the kiosk on the brink

vending cans of molten sugar, dreadful trade,
then wound back down by the parched red track
to the car park where the gypsy woman sat

with those chunks of pyrite, fool's gold, fire
cooled, cast and cubed in the dire forge.

Flood

The mountain dug its heels into the draff
that ran from its sides in ropes of gravel
as the black pearls of rain hit off the rock.

Then the sea moved in to meet the mountain's flow
and overstepped the concrete mole and wrecked
the beach-huts, the football pitch, the sandwich stall

and scaled the doorsteps and the windowsills
where it came to rest. Along that level
the bay and the square were a seamless cope

the tops of the tallest cars kept just above
while their owners circled them in rowboats
and, half its height, the square's one palm tree

rode the ripples through that inland sea
with the air of a battered periscope.

Earthquake

Inside the mountain earth begins to move
its joints and spring the links that pegged it down
– the fans of schist, the chocks and wedges of

feldspar and chert. A daylight owl screws back
from rock that spilling derelicts her nest
then quiet plugs the ear, a twist of wax.

Behind the quiet a core of silence hums
until earth moves again – this time in earnest:
dumb matter's rigid-tongued delirium

wrung at the verge of the crack that gapes at
the heart of things, that widens the Norman watchtower
from its sunken gateway to the parapet

as the tide uncoils. This means in Purgatory
a soul pinned to the rock has broken free

Lengths of Air

The mountain had its shoulders in the cloud
it kept its head above, rich folds of cloud
with tassels spilling round a clump of rock.

Above the cloud a village like a wasps' nest
in fractured soapy pinks and crusted honey
hung on to nothing by a thread

and from its topmost balcony a woman
let out the rope that let her basket down
past the cloud, the winding road, the lemon groves

in their black nets and down the mountainside
until it reached sea-level where I knelt
and found inside the photo and the note.

I trembled at that nakedness and read:
here I am on my bed inlaid with lapis.

Hortus Conclusus

The Reptilarium has parked under the palm tree
like an Ark on wheels, a seething caravan
it costs no more than the news to enter.

Tomorrow we can read about the world
but today we'll wander back to origin
and see through glass what took Eve's breath away

and gave it back quickened. The sleepy snakes
lie wreathed around themselves or slither through
the hoops of their own skin, their hanks of hemp.

A tongue or a mouse's tail retracts within
the lipless smile of a green tree python.
Such heavy necklaces! So far from Eden!

The driver counts the coins into his tin.
The sun curls its last rays round the mountain.

The Return

This is the indelible place you lived in.
There's no mistaking the scales of moonlight
on the stucco though the fertile gutters

are only shadows, some windows have been lost,
some scarred with fire and the kiosk selling
cut watermelons and contraband tobacco

has lapsed. You try to ignore the gaps around
your memory palace: the statue of Neptune
that served to hide a patch of turquoise sea;

the convent which in your time was a brothel.
A team of builders from the coast are still
plastering the vaults of the vestibule

which even with scaffolding are out of reach.
Now you take the street inside the palace
and turn left down some worn steps into night

where the walls jostle you and brush your arm
with whitewash. You stand at the iron door
to calm yourself then turn the iron key

and face the next door. You're sure that everything
will now be as it was and hardly look
till you reach the long room: pale green damask

is pouring off the bed in dark green folds.
The balcony is frail and higher than you thought
but looks down on the unchanged saffron flowers

of the pomegranate tree. Late summer comes.
The beige trunk, twisting, leans its topmost branch
onto the rail and offers you the last fruit,

its rind burst by the crush of cells,
and holding it out to light your way you leave
again determined to mislay the key.

Sirensong

Why do you think he went on wandering
after the orchestrated pathos of his homecoming
– the hot bath, the clean sheets, the postal code?

It wasn't that he was bored by his wife;
more she by him and by those years of waiting
(for what?) with better prospects close at hand.

It wasn't as he pretended the desire
to travel to the edge of the known world
where he could found some godforsaken waste.

Lashed to the mast, did he think the wax
he'd also plugged his own ears with would work?
And that the siren's downcast eyes expressed

the fear she'd lost him not the lack of doubt
her voice would carry till it found him out?

Skin Deep

The headlamps of divers
cast a greasy cloud of light just under
the sea's dark skin. Before you can blink

the octopus has played a symphony
of russet stipples and black bands
across its back. It thinks in colour.

Beware and welcome have twenty inflections
like Delacroix saying Mon cher monsieur
– for tomorrow's lunch they'll all boil down

to an inky sauce, some Redon lithograph
of spiders dancing in the afterlife.

Uroboros

I was partway outside a takeaway pizza napoletana
watching tv when the bone of an anchovy
stuck in my throat – a neat posthumous deterrent.
An eight-legged tag team tangled with the ropes
to the sound of squeezed ribs and pummelled rubber.
I switched to a thing on the mangrove swamps:
crabs eating muck, frogs eating crabs, snakes
eating frogs ... So who eats the snakes? The snakes
eat themselves at the top of the food-chain
out of habit or boredom or sheer bravado.
It's a world of mud out there and you have to
like it to survive though even if you like it
no one's saying you survive for long.
What's that fish, the yokker fish or something,
that lurks and spits a crystal arc that knocks
the ants off overhanging blades of grass? There's no
safety in numbers, in looking insignificant or vile.
You can't say, Don't mind me, I'm nothing special
and basically I taste of toenails. A taste for you
yoked to some gimmick for hunting you down
has been stalking through millennia intent
on the delicate dread of your last gasp.
It's a world of mud and guts out there. My advice
is don't be anything stupid like a shrimp
and evolve yourself a tooth- and claw-proof vest
and stay wedged deep in a burrow all your life,
if you call it a life, like the solitary mud lobster,
ugly as truth and glum as a lumpsucker,
which seemingly without moving somehow keeps going
for it's a mystery how they get to mate.

Frankenstein's Pre-natal Recollections

The place of origin was emptiness
and fine metallic dust with lines
of bunsen burners burning nothing
or clearing their throats of filaments
and solder – blue-flecked black flames
sepulchral as cypresses. The air was utterly
exhaled, through-other like the name
we acquired, a cast-off from the doctor.
We thought we had been someone/something
else before, sought out like truffles
under lanterns and then swathed
in cellars; but that was before 'before'
and is a thought at best patched up.
Better to start with the gloomy angel
hunched over slide-rules and a rheostat
and those two galvanic shining spheres

fire linked – we felt fire stitch the air
and scatter filings in dark iron wings
and our heart leaped to the spark, one fell
precipitant connecting like Paganini
off on some solo. Our own right arm
which props our chin in this reflective mood
bears the pale papery stitched-up mark
of reaching through a glass door to escape
indoors, out of the agoraphobic garden
where rows of flowers array themselves
in threads not even Solomon . . .
but so unstriven-for we really wonder
what keeps them at it. For us each movement

is an impossible bridging of fault-lines,
each thought unprecedented as a tripod
which must learn to dance upon a tightrope.

Stood Up

The clock turns bulbous, fish-eyed, whiskery.
The longlegged clock-hands take scissory strides
above you. Darts spring back from the jumbled dial,
pointedly snubbed, while you still wait

for a breathless explanation that would lift,
as a seal lifts a beachball, the dead weight
of your chin, of the hours, propped on your arm's
Dalì stilt now that the clock has melted

in pools of spilt beer islanding the ashtray
and only the wind judders the swingdoors
or else some stranger. Half-stewed, old droopy-jaws

who winds the grizzled ends of his moustache
might well be you, but ten year on, still waiting
for love to walk in before closing time.

Home Thoughts

The airmail from India, a weatherbeaten blue,
with wax marks from the candle you had used
to write by reached me. You write that reach
is what travellers there do rather than arrive
being more respectful to the gods of place.
For years your letters from around the world
have kept on reaching me wherever
I'm hunched beside an atlas and a lamp.
When you last saw me I was living in a room
across the road from but a floor below
the room we used to share ten years ago.
Only kindness stopped you saying
it took me quite some time to cross that road;
and looking from my window I expect to see
myself looking out to where in ten years time
I'll be looking back again to see ... the last things
you mention are the Parsee towers of silence
where the dead are left for vultures to attend.
I warm to that. It sort of brings things home.

The Master Stroke
for Xon de Ros

The hair stands on end and waits to be split
   by the heft of the little axeman.
The two halves peel the length of the hairshaft
to the applause of two ladies-in-waiting
whose calves are like four table legs.
The hair that's split is split again.
   That's not a hair the axeman says,
it's a silk thread, a grass blade, the moth's antennae.

I dream at night beside the wedge-shaped tower,
   a glass axe buried in the earth.
Inside the column built inside the tower
they split a single atom into halves
then both halves have to spend their halflives
seeking the other half they'll never find.
   That's not an atom the axeman says,
it's a misprint, a mutant, the mote in your eye.

Above, Below

Suspicion

straight as a signpost
planted in space
the angel Uriel
kept watch on the heights

his four wings
of fiery quartz
made the glottal clack
of magpies or castanets

when asked which way
his arm replied
*That spot to which I point
is paradise*

and what if a devil
in passing had swivelled
his faithfulness
one eighty degrees

Sleight of Hand

just a sly shove
and the chipped angel
will plummet down
into the brambles

where I caught you
red-handed
with a bucketful
of blackberries

so that they fell
among your clothes
where there's time enough
for us to find them

hearing the bees tread
the sunflower's heart
their back legs
barrelled with gold

Mortal Remains

below the blue arrow
of the one way sign
above the harvest
of a street bin
the two tone
zinc
of a pigeon's wing
or Franciscan cassock
next to where a green
and ochre sticker depicting
a baffled rat declares
*this street has been
deratted* there's
a pale square
from which a funeral
poster has been torn
down leaving
only
a black border
with no lettering –
someone called something
Esposito
if I remember
right *was gathered up
into the realm of angels*

Inheritance

By prudence, integrity and diligence,
the Latin virtues, he had worked his way
from 'nothing' to those heights from which
it wouldn't take us long to fall. He left me
no blueprints and no climbing gear to haul
me back to solvency though I received
his christian name and surname
and dutifully plagiarized his signature
off the Isle of Man three-legged one-pound note.
Chief General Manager of Martins Bank:
his title had the decimal prestige
of a pentameter, of the rattle of beads
on an abacus, but was not hereditary.

I was however once invited to
the Liverpool Head Office, a temple
of trading ringed by gilded iron spikes
and the finial crockets of acanthus.
The manager led us down into the vault
where gold bars from Johannesburg were wheeled
about on trolleys; then up through a skylight
to the parapet above the dome. From there
the kingdoms of the city spread beneath us
rickety with fire escapes and aerials,
all blackened brick and base metals:
bombsites, dockyards, the Mersey's pimpled zinc.
Between us and nothing, the lowest of handrails.

The bank's emblem was a grasshopper
with back legs triggered to unleash the bulk
of its blunt brow and plated thorax.
We had one as a gold paperweight poised

on a black plinth and another
squatting in the porch to prize off boots
with plaques of rust at its poll and wingcase.
Soon enough it would chirr in the crop of an eagle
when Barclays took over in a corporate merger.

Here there was a family history to be traced:
Martins had merged with the Bank of Liverpool
which years before in turn had joined
the firm of Arthur Heywood who had made
his pile from ships that plied the Gold
and Windward Coasts, Old Callabar, Benin...
A thousand leg-irons fixed to their quarterdecks,
those boats were christened with bright abstract names:
Integrity, Providence, Friendship, Liberty.

A Small Flag
for Lucie Oldham

I'd barely finished painting and had meant to send
this mountain, less a mountain than a molehill
with a village at its foot and a village way up
but too faint to believe in, a hopeless idyll,

when news came of your death. The envelope
has stayed unstuck, unstamped, and void, and here,
now not one of your old addresses is any help
and no stamp on earth will see it past the border.

I thought of your arrival in Liverpool
in '68 when you entered the house as our new sister.
It was then I first heard of Dubček and Svoboda
and pinned a small enamel flag to my lapel.

You must have found our vicarious nationalism
quaint as a cloakroom, a far cry from Prague
and our lives by the oily river oddly tranquil
between the stolid hedge and the burgherly backwall.

Last time I saw you, in the restaurant,
you were thinner and paler, your eyes
unaltered and your voice a torrent
swerving between the disastrous and the humorous.

I still catch your accent, travelling backwards,
knocking the usual patterns of speech awry
to open meanings in the hearts of words,
ironic and mobile in their sleeves of air.

Ancient History

The year began with baleful auguries:
comets, eclipses, tremors, forest fires,
the waves lethargic under a coat of pitch
the length of the coastline. And a cow spoke,
which happened last year too, although last year
no one believed cows spoke. Worse was to come.
There was a bloody rain of lumps of meat
which flocks of gulls snatched in mid-air
while what they missed fell to the ground
where it lay for days without festering.
Then a wind tore up a forest of holm-oaks
and jackdaws pecked the eyes from sheep.
Officials construing the Sibylline books
told of helmeted aliens occupying
the crossroads, and high places of the city.
Blood might be shed. Avoid, they warned,
factions and in-fights. The tribunes claimed
this was the usual con-trick
trumped up to stonewall the new law
about to be passed. Violence was only curbed
by belief in a rumour that the tribes
to the east had joined forces and forged
weapons deadlier than the world has seen
and that even then the hooves of their scouts
had been heard in the southern hills.
The year ended fraught with the fear of war.
Next year began with baleful auguries.

Matador

He left that bull of a man to bleed
at the dead end of the granite puzzle
and by winding spider's silk on a cotton reel
got the hell out – the first to do so, thanks
to the brute's half-sister, the mistress who'd
masterminded his escape. For reward
he took her off to Naxos, and there he dumped her.
No great shame, as anyway the wine god
had just drawn up in his leopardskin caravan
but it gives you some idea about our man.

While snapping shut the pleats of his scarlet cape
in a media veronica for the crew's applause
the last thing on his mind were those black sails.
But at landfall – the name exact – he saw
a vague figure hang in the updraft for an age
against the cliffs and waited for the noise,
dark-centred and spray-edged, to flower inside him.
Only then did the thought come home
that the death of the monster in the maze
was never the real object of his voyage.

Paestum

The three temples are like things with roots
that channel the weather into bedrock
and pulse with a low frequency way under earshot
earth rumours back into the stratosphere.

The uttermost limit of the Grand Tour,
its point of exhaustion and refreshment,
the travertine stonework rises like a
shimmering wall of sea although the sea

and its god have withdrawn from sight behind
the polished cubits of the perimeter wall
leaving the harbour stranded. Malaria
filled the spaces where the sea had been,

and shifting trade-routes and the tilt of power
and a black rain of lapilli
left this stone unroofed and tenantless, the haunt
by day of jackdaws and by night of owls.

Snakes that pose under the famous roses
at the edge of wedding photos last year claimed
a satin bride for Dis. The Doric columns
tower in TV adverts and tourist brochures

while the triglyphs still grip the entablature
like talons. On the diver's tomb in the museum
earth swells and might as well be water under
the silent leap of the diver

– his body finding itself in mid-flight
suddenly supple again and childlike, arched,
his weight assumed by air which any moment might
spring wide like the Sea Gate onto a burning source.

[69]

Vehicle

I jolt awake at the wheel of this wreck
   made of resin, crystals and cracked amber,
its dashboard dial a compass pointing south.

All the things I ever had and kept –
   old files, old coats and age-old daily papers,
smudged and piss-yellow, fly out the rear-window

   unravelling and tearing in the backdraught
   and snagging on the dark umbrella pines
that line the coast now that the rocks have turned

   to the sand we glimpse when the wood gives way
   to trees. The mozzarella buffalo are chewing
lumps of earth and barely lift their heavy heads

   to watch us. The hard shoulder's a fur-rack
   of flattened stoats and moles and the odd dog
lying among pools of oil and shattered bodywork.

We pass the dead city with its four gates,
   three temples and twice-flowering roses;
then the one stall selling painted urns and postcards.

A black-haired woman stands by the road
   in a tight lowcut black crape dress –
for miles the wind brings lovely skeins and pockets of

   her spikenard perfume through the former windscreen
   with flakes of darkness which we wipe away
like ash-filled cobwebs or swart veils of lace.

And as the sun drops to the lacquered sea
   it's hard to figure out how long the car
can hold together, given the speed it's going,

or how long it's been since we set out
trailing tiny shining cubes of glass
and scattering scraps of everything I've owned

past so many earthworks and abandoned
homes that now it seems I'm staring
out at the Pole Star through a window of bone.

A Roman Ruin

RIP Wolseley 1500, MOT
failure cum laude, rust-plaqued, cough-racked jade,
eyesore, ossiary, tin tub, dustbin
– that last oil can was your extreme unction.

What's left can be my memento mori
or a monument to Britain's now decayed
industrial base. There's a sepia postcard
bluetacked to your walnut dashboard

of the ruined palace of one Septimus
– weeds feasting off its arches much as moss
(some rolling stone) does on your window rim.

O pilgrim, you who search for Rome in Rome...
Forget it. Neither the Tiber nor the Thames
will be graced again by your ancient chrome.

Boneshaker

for Bernard O'Donoghue

'Is it about a bicycle,' he asked. – Flann O'Brien

My not having read *The Third Policeman*
left the piece I'd meant to write on bicycles
seriously under-researched, to put it politely,

as you did, but even before that crucial omission
the whole idea was a non-starter given
I'd never recollect with anything like

tranquillity the strong emotion I experienced
when some sly thief under cloak of darkness
coaxed my racer from the plastic drainpipe

I'd chained it to. No matter that it cost a fiver
from a Hackney scrapyard whose curator
sat throned on an armchair which long ago

may have looked less like a padded dishrag.
Feed the cats, he growled at his thin crony
who began to saw in half an industrial can

of whalemeat while their nine cats, nine lives apiece,
that's as many as eighty-one lives, converged on him
like a raddled orchestra of shofars.

I saw the bike at once and lifted it sky-high
with the distal phalanx of my little finger.
It was as light as a bird not as a feather

like Valéry suggested the true poem should be.
Its lightness was such that it must have been stolen
even then, or especially then, but I eyed it

as Phaeton must have eyed his father's chariot.
I can see you're straight up, the man told my friend
and then (as if aware he'd left me out)

I'm not saying that you're a villain.
But wheels don't come as narrow as those wheels are.
You could pawn that pushbike in a piss-hole.

Eh? Without more words I paid hard cash
but the next day going down the Ball's Pond Road
on that brace of shakes with its shaky brakes

I achieved an unrehearsed forwards roll
across a windscreen the way those Cretan girls
would flip over the horns of a bull, which as

Picasso noticed were the shape of handlebars
but that story's been told. One life later,
the man who'd scythed me down was whistling:

The speed you were going was more like the wind
than the wind itself, an image
he must have known would more than make amends

for the fact that the bike was never quite the same
with a crotchety click at its cotter-pin
and a kerbward-biased front wheel which wore down

one breakblock like a shauchled heel though still
it was fleet as Achilles and a sight less warlike,
being one of mankind's few benign inventions

though the truth is I can't help but hope
it's been far from benign to the one who stole it.
May he bruise his shins – ouch – on those pedals.

The Spleen Factory

after Carlos Drummond de Andrade

I want to make a sonnet that's not a sonnet
according to any civilized notion of what
that is. I want it ugly as concrete,
and just about impossible to read.

And I'd like my sonnet in the future
to give no living soul an ounce of pleasure,
not by being merely foulmouthed and perverse
but also (why not?) by being both and worse

if it feels the urge. Plus I want the whole thing caustic
and obtrusive – with intent to pierce and hurt
like stitches done without anaesthetic

somewhere tender. So it won't be learnt by heart.
So it's a wall with a hole pissed through – in the hole a star
transmitting incomprehensible clarity.

The One-Star
for Michael Hofmann

Moving away in the taxi, I could just see myself
    climbing the marble steps and stepping through
    the plate-glass into a lounge-cum-vestibule,

its floor inlaid with a pink star of mineral grains
    and roughage – a breakfast for the afterlife.
    Beaded oak cladding, electrified oil-lamps,

a pharaonic desk-clerk. The air was cut and dried
    as though reconstituted in the basement's lungs
    and laid out, and folded, in cool dry reams.

The Shining was obtainable on the video service
    but would be scrambled after several minutes
    if you failed to press the 'Confirm' button

– otherwise it was a sex film I was embarrassed
    for the glamorous Thai receptionist
    to know I was watching. So I tried to read

The Temptation to Exist feeling conspicuously
    absent and uneasily aware
    of being ironed flat, flatter, by the clean sheets

and of the bedside table's inbuilt clock
    with its defective digits: every minute
    was a minus sign or a gnomon, every hour

was missing a slant side to its parallelogram.
    I closed the eyelids of the two nightlights;
    then mine ... until I woke as though I'd feasted

on finely-ground enamel. There was nothing for it
   but to go home – some home! – but first why not
   spirit away the bar of opalescent soap, the small

urn of bath-foam and the shroud-sewing kit
   the size of a matchbook, with loops of thread
   five different shades of grey

or maybe it was the light? I had a good mind
   to mend the inside lining of my coat
   but instead went down in the shiny lift

and sank in an armchair by the crystal ashtray.
   Was I a Mr John Ashbery, someone asked me.
   No, I replied, not Mr Ashbery

– but pausing mysteriously mid-sentence as I felt
   he deserved a couple more guesses for being
   somehow on the right track, if not exactly warm.

The pause obviously disturbed him. He didn't
   like that pause. Well tell him
   if you'd be so kind that his taxi's waiting.

Oh yes I could just see myself doing that.

The Marble Fly

The guide crinkled his nose
like a squirrel with a nut
as he pointed out to us
the baked-clay phallus
on the oven door, no doubt
symbolic of the risen loaf.

Red dust and stone thresholds
to an unrecovered world,
stone fruit that Felix
the fruitseller sold, stone-cold
drinks from the hot drinks stall,
wheel ruts cut in the stone road.

Murals, mosaics, mysteries:
the pierced stag, the girl's back
exposed to the beaded whip,
a lion mauling the shift of Thisbe
whilst a wall-eyed Pyramus
has severed an artery.

A wall relief in the Wool Market
shows the animal world in marble
– a lizard can-opening a cricket,
a mouse airlifted by an owl
and a fly (watch out, fly!)
on its own among the bulrushes –

all perfectly preserved and just
a shade larger than lifesize
and much stiller than life and harder.

It can't have been long after
that much the same idea
occurred to Vesuvius.

Span

Eye-level with the alps of ash and slag
I trawl my floor for a BT counterfoil
deep into its scarlet monitory phase
through shards and rags and scraps
and rivelled gold tobacco threads and these
long white hairs which must be mine
alas as no one else
would venture into this rented room
except one short-haired black-haired cat.
And here's a flea he carried on his back,
a tiny emissary from the caliphat
of bad dreams, doing vaults and back-flips
onto three golden dusters, bought last year
and still sealed in polythene,
their hems blanket-stitched with crimson thread
in a series of small 'v's overlapping
the dictionary. Crimson: it burns a fuse
the length of a dusty trail of roots
back to Arabic: qirmizi:
meaning the Scarlet Grain insect which breeds
on the kermes oak – stuff Solomon hung
beneath the wrought-gold
five-cubit wingspan of the cherubim . . .
Crimson lights up back along the line of
the trade-routes west, at each camel-stop
or port – a vowel-shift, a letter
dislodged from the throat to the palate
colouring the sound. My eyes lift
to the level of the window, facing east
onto brickwork, tarmac and slate tiles.
Upon the windowsill – a fly's black torso,

deep in the mire of last year's dust,
with its seraph wings still poised for flight
but cumbersome like panes
of leaded glass or paddles of cracked quartz,
tired for a while of beating at the air.

The Duet

From the eaves of the room I live in
comes a din as parliamentary and relentless
as windscreen wipers on a dry windscreen
– tremulous ballads to domestic bliss
which rarely get beyond the first failed line.
But then the clatter of my electric Canon,
its pinhead headbutting the daisywheel,
will stop them gargling gravel for a while.

It's at it again, their silence might be saying,
it's nature's joke the way those creatures sing.
And, as hardly ever, if it should go on
over the page an indignant pigeon,
that's my excuse, rakes the gutter with its claws
and creaks into flight like a rusty hinge.

Flight

for Valerie Lipman

spruce hickory bamboo
(though only for a few seconds)
the first aircraft flew

as if the wind had a mind
to clear the air of any weather
that might tilt the scales
one way or the other

as the tenons quaked
and the dowelling screaked
and the single rear rudder

came to grief
like the tail
or tailfeather
of an unfledged hippogriff.

Flying Colours

In a terracotta field in Catalonia
I help a small boy set his kite aloft
though neither of us has a notion how
it's meant to work, the wind – the tramontana that lifts

the white dust from the hoofmarks on the dirt-track
and crinkles an earthbound beetle's wingcase
after vaulting the peaks of the Pyrenees –
knows enough for both of us and hoiks

the heraldic disc with its long tail of cellophane
out and up, taut then slack then taut once more,
unlooping the nylon cord which at a certain
height vanishes into thin air like gossamer

and the boy calls out *¡mira la cometa como va!*
though it looks to me like it needs
a new name – not kite, not comet ... Some odd idea
happily going nowhere in a series of nods,

swerves, shrugs, juts, rips, spins and figures-of-eight
so, unsure which is near or far, or up or down,
he and I are nothing but the place the kite
has chosen us to anchor on

as gusts riffle the sweetcorn's papery sheaves
and pluck at the kermes oaks and pylon wires
and we marvel at the tiny planet attached to us
– its jagged flight,
                              its deep unearthly colours.

A Flight of Locks

I *Flow*

The Greek who said you can never
step into the same river
twice hadn't dreamt of

the slow seepage of canals
with their oil and graphite sheen,
liquid packed solid as a pencil lead

where time is cased in a long cabinet
stowed with the ownerless archives
of two centuries of weather,

the lump of coal from Warwickshire,
the tipcat, the fender, the bleached horse's tail
once tied to a painted tiller.

II *Canal*

The wheels of perpetual motion
have ground to a halt
or almost a halt

while underwater on the bed
of puddled clay
packhorses trod down watertight

in that sedgy trench of slime
lies the frayed peak of a navvy's cap
beside a copper

cartwheel twopenny-bit, its rim
incised with 1 7 9 7
around the frogspawn jowls of George the Third.

III *Canalside*

The fishers sit beside
the giant on its back
with their chests-of-drawers

packed with quills of peacock, crow
and porcupine for floats and bait
of maggots, casters, hempseed, wheat,

hearing the water's sluggish flow
like a flywheel ticking, a lunar tug
from the summit down the flight of locks

to the headwaters of the tidal river
– quiet as the perch's crimson fin
that surfaces and disappears.

IV *Lock*

At the crank of the windlass in the racks
the paddle boards' square blocks of elm
are lifted in the lock head like two eyelids

so water sluices through the culverts
on either side of the lock's brick chamber
in swags and scallops and volutes

burled and blurred and bossed and scooped
like a crystal maelstrom in a bottleneck
crizzling its uprush in a double ridge

till risen it overrides itself
and the sky resembles its reflection
on the stilled upheaval of one level.

v *Heron*

Dead-centre down the still canal
a blue ghost flies with a mussel shell
clamped lightly in its bill

folding the daybreak's river mist
with the creaking steps of its flight
past the diamonds and daisies on the cratch

of the narrowboat
clove-hitched to a cast-iron bollard,
past the dredger's hopper, the humpbacked bridge

then drops the empty shell
still hinged by a thread
among flints and ashkeys on the tow-path.

vi *Bridge*

The humpbacked bridge
is taking umbrage
and making a bright hoop

of its bricklined arch
like a dancer's sturdy instep
on the unbroken surface

where the quilled stumps
of pollard willows
shiver like the steel bristles

on a flea's armour
or rest, head-down, like sable
brushes in a jar of turps.

In the Hold

Route-marching, field-postcards, tents hung with scrim
– we waited in those Domesday parishes
for D-Day to begin.

Beyond the wood there was a flint-harled church
and a watertower like a missile in plainclothes
– a tall tube with a concrete hat on top.

I can still feel the pink rim the beret left
embossed on my receded hairline
and the veins in my forehead swelling

with the notes of the bird I couldn't see
bubbling like water through a sea-vent
while darkness linked the leaves and thickened.

From Suffolk they drove us down by night
to the New Forest where we were nearer still
the zero-hour

that months of training had prepared us for
not thinking too far ahead of or about
by filling the days with strict inspections.

And then the lorry drive in convoy
to the blunt-hulled landing ships,
the gangplank a small step from the footboard.

Once in the hold I heard the air compress
as the round steel hatch was clamped down shut
and tightened by a half-turn on the hand-grips

and there we all were in the dim light that came on
stowed in the hollow belly of the war
– a box that clanged and stank of diesel –

till daylight heaped us on the other shore.

Ultima Thule

On a family outing to the final island,
wobblingly tall, the fools of ocean, together
we rode the rubber dinghy. Our father manned

the stunted paddles, blade on the feather,
regardless of the waves chilled from world's end.
The black hexagonal basalt columns reared

like a row of crayons worn down at different
rates from scribbling on the ether,
the nearest – pedestals for cormorants.

Like weathervanes, the rowlocks slithered round.
The boat floor pumped and tussled like a heart
sculpting our insteps with its upthrust as

the island rowed itself away from us,
towering at the edge of time forever.

Banana Boat

'I wasn't born on a banana boat yesterday'
the porter told us (not that we'd asked)
when we tried to bluff our way without a pass
into the Liverpool University Pool.
He growled then waved us through the turnstile
with a wink as good as a season ticket.
Did he know me from somewhere, or just think he did?

As for me, I wasn't born in a bungalow.
I was, come to think of it – not so much born
as put together, the main piece fitting into place
when we moved to a house above the Mersey
and the concrete rampart of Garston Docks,
the barbed-wire and the pill-box from the war
– the main piece, or so I'd like to think.

But if Pat Cassidy wasn't born, as he said
he wasn't, on one of Fyffe's banana boats
which from the Albert Dock used to supply
the whole country with bananas (except during the war)
that didn't rule out he might have been born
on some other boat like a vessel stacked
with iron-bound trunks of Swedish pine

on their way to be axed into matchsticks
at Bryant & May's factory down the road,
or in the hold of a ship from Trinidad
full of sugar cane for Tate & Lyle's.
Certainly there was something
scouse-maritime about him – an old hulk
moored to a sandbank on the river.

He made me think of the one heirloom I had
(from my mother's father I'd never met) –
a Bermuda-rig model yacht plank-built
by Mr Rawlinson, his friend, the docker,
and of the foghorns' shindy on New Year's Eve
when the boat-lights blazed at the stroke of twelve
where Sassoon had dumped his Military Cross.

Still, whether on one or another sort of boat,
at sea or in dry dock, no one would dispute
that Corporal Cassidy, who had (I found out)
served beside my father in the Second,
admittedly, and not the First World War
– no one would dispute he wasn't born yesterday
though his cheeks were as pink as if he was.

Survival

as the crew sang
a capstan shanty
adapted by
Barbadians
from an Irish tune

the ten-gun brig
hove to
beside a cherty rock
in mid-Atlantic
only occupied

by crabs and lichen
and nesting colonies
of the booby
and the noddy
– *of such a tame*

and stupid disposition
the naturalist recalled
I could have killed
any number of them
with my geological hammer

– there in a nutshell
he'd hit on
the origin
of the Origin
and the twilight of Species

Taken Awares

I fall into every trap
they set for me —
mantrap, mousetrap, birdlime.

Every time
I take the bait —
the worm, the cheese, whatever.

I pluck the wire
that shifts the lever
that springs the teeth.

Then, in the calm before death,
I flatter myself
I'd seen it all a mile off.

I even manage a small laugh.

Six Characters in Search of Something

A friend of mine met the son of a man
who it seems was eaten by a polar bear
in Iceland where the bear had stepped ashore
rafted from Greenland on an ice-floe.

The father of the man who met my friend
saw the bear who'd eat him loitering near
the shore and hurried on and met another man
who was walking the other way towards the bear.

He gave that other man his walking stick
but the bear meanwhile had doubled back
and reappeared on the path ahead
of the man who now was unprotected.

There may be a moral in this story
for the man, his son, the man he met,
for my friend, for me, or even for the bear,
but if there is it's better left unsaid.

Name-Tag

Every sock and collar has a name-tag.
I have a name, a surname, and a tartan rug
with tassels. What else? A zip-up
pigskin letterwriting-case that's pitted
where the bristles have been scorched away.
Once a week we write neat letters home with
our marks and team scores which the master reads.
Mornings, we get a tick for shitting
after the prefect has inspected it.
Through the keyhole old MacMillan
is sitting on his single bed
and talking to the service revolver
he uses with blanks to start the races.
Our toes are fat red bulbs from chilblains.
Already one skin has rubbed away, another grown
harder than the first, a kind of pigskin.
We must never sneak or blub or suck up.
We wear steel studs that spark. Scoured lugs
stick out from crew cuts as we learn by heart
the Latin for pitching camp and waging war
and the psalm where I am made
to lie down in green pastures and a table
is prepared for me and my enemies.
The tables are mopped with swab rags,
the dustbins tipped among the ferns
and bamboo of the watergarden
for this was once a country house
and we are lucky to enjoy the fine grounds
which we see through the barred windows
or on Sunday walks trying to keep up
with the master who ran the marathon.

In the wooden locker by the metal bed
I have a chipped enamel mug,
a toothbrush, a comb, a nailbrush and two shoebrushes
with which, with time, I could scrub away
my shoes, my nails, my hair, my teeth –
given time enough, the buildings, the pitches,
the gate's ironwork with its clawing lion
and all we've learnt till nothing's left
but the Blasted Oak I carved my name on
and perhaps the derelict pavilion.

Person Unknown

It remembers me still the time I left
with a kilim bag sewn to a hessian strip

which held the fresh pad and the pen-knife to cut
a reed pen from a bed of bulrushes

and for the time being the one pyramid
bottle of waterproof Chinese Stick ink

inside. Since then has anything occurred
to change the shapes I meant to make?

I passed an unknown person on the road
wearing red shoes with coiled rope soles.

The ink dried mauve in tiny alps of grit.
The knife broke. The book yellowed. The bag frayed

holding on by a few plumed threads
then snapped and left my shoulders set

and warped against the phantom weight
of thin air that hasn't forgotten me yet.

Gainful Employment

As if I had nothing better to do,
and who says I have, than putting the house
I haven't got in order, I sit at the oak desk
I have got, though really a table not a desk
but it's mine and I sanded it down myself
and beeswaxed it with iron wire-wool

— that was how important it was for me:
this surface on which so much was to be
accomplished. Best of all, I can take
its legs off, and replace them by way of
four angelic wing-nuts to the corner brackets
so it's both a steadfast and a movable beast.

But I wonder why I kept this biro spring
I'm exercising now between my finger
and thumb — not to sew my eyelids up with
like the envious spirits in purgatory.
Just too exquisite to throw away,
an image of infinity or information...

I'm still here, where there's an unconsolable
joy to be had, sitting ready at my station
and waiting for the bugle or the slughorn.
No one can say it's wasting time, my time, the time I've got,
to enter the very thread of the helix,
to live always expecting the unheard of.

Illuminated Manuscript

The Master of the Entangled Figures
has penned me in the curl of a worm's tail,
a weirdly ribbed and beaded spiral
inside the U of the word VIR
at the head of The Book of Job's first verse.
Soon as I'd set foot in the Land of Uz
I watched him bite his tongue to stop it
rushing ahead of the script, a laborious
thicket of Latin in which each capital
is pressed out like blue from a stone. No doubt
I'll come to accept my entanglement
like a mute owl on an ivy tod
though now I can hardly tell
where my limbs begin and his letters end.

Possession

This patch of green attached to the rented house
belongs to the clutches of the ivy
I've begun (what's got into me?)
to rip from the sycamore trunk it's clamped on
and from the lawn where its cables,
like supply-lines, are dug in
through bronchial roots, and bear an iron code:
extend, secure. It tears the skin from my fingers,
expressing a thin milk, probably poison.
In one afternoon, I've undone seasons
of reinforcement, of slow dominion
as though I had a new law to dispense.

As though I had some hanging-gardens in mind.
But the verminous life-forms it's helped
advance: spiders, woodlice and snails that creep,
at their respective paces, back and away
in search of cover. The earth itself
seems dank and affronted, and a death's-head moth
foxes my eyelids like a page of Euclid
– all painted dust, bristling and admonitory.
Soon enough I'll be tangled up like Laocoön
on the compost heap, my wrists and ankles bound,
and the small creatures will be at home in me
and my mouth will sprout a glossy angular leaf.

A Shortened History in Pictures

The Child Maximilian in a White Frock.
The Imperial Family with their Chairs and Pet Cat.
Maximilian, a Thoughtful Young Man in Black.
Maximilian, Emperor of Mexico, at Court.
The Empress of Mexico, his Wife Charlotte.
The Emperor Maximilian on Horseback.
Maximilian and his Court Playing Cricket
(with the English Ambassador, Sir Charles Wyke).

The Broken Cacti and the Convent's Outer Wall.
The Execution Squad Standing to Attention.
A Mestizo Leading a Llama under Popocatépetl.
The Execution of Miramón, Mejía and Maximilian.
The Gold-Green Tail-Feathers of the Quetzal.
The Emperor's Shirt after his Execution.

The Century Plant

A century after its introduction
to Oxford's Botanic Gardens greenhouse,
on the site of the medieval Jewish cemetery,
the agave has taken a leap of faith
it won't survive, and begun to blaze
with sulphurous buds. It's not clear whether
global or more local warming lit the fuse
in the patient rootstock and sent one limb
rocketing upward so its top
can look down even on the banana tree
besides the other transplants. The palm-line
is said to move a metre north each year
– these days more like a kilometre –
but either way the agave's too far ahead
to be caught up with, despite the hundred years
of waiting – now two, at the most three weeks
of prodigal flowering and the whole thing ends.

In 1850 in Seville,
while his contemporaries photographed
rotting barges on the Guadalquivir
or farm labourers in sheepskin waistcoats
or gypsy women in the tobacco factory,
Vicomte J. de Vigier
turned his back on the folkloric and his lens
on the common-or-garden naturalized exotics
like palm trees and bamboo. His masterpiece,
Etude d'aloès, shows this tumid
dusty plant on a nondescript roadside.
It holds grimly on to its patch of nowhere
and drinks and drinks the silver nitrate light

as though there were no belonging anywhere
but there and then, and nothing sublime
except that stretch of dirt, that broken wall
and the rays of a faded nineteenth-century sun.

Gardener's World

Yes, we're in the potting-shed again this week
with Mr Jones among the seedlings...
his wrinkles have dug in, his intellectual fingers
are a dark pollen-coated mothy umber.
He's in, he's always in, his overcoat
which when he moves gives off a sweetened cloud
of twine and potash like a hardware store.

The owners of the garden where he works
have kept a special mug for his own use
called Jonesies Mug, though no one else
would dream of using it. He sips the tea,
the florid healthy colour of flowerpots,
while muttering to the calyx of a small tomato:
Well, the Missis is a bit under the weather today.

– A figure of speech that falls a fraction short.
Right now she's barricading their front door
with thousands of cans of catfood
she'd stockpiled in the cellar against
the years of famine. He shrugs and walks away
like a dazed tortoise in the stiff panels
of his coat then stoops into the boiler-house

which stores his various implements besides
an explained medicine-ball like a prize pumpkin.
His cup of tea has turned as cold as stone.
And now he's ambled way beyond the rockery.
And now he's gone – the cracked furry boots
and the creases of his pass-the-parcel face
are lost forever out among the lupins.

On/Off

The switch stuck through the lampstand's neck
like an arrow shaft of walrus ivory
in a Welsh epic
has lost its feathers and its head.
Peacock feathers and a gold head.
Its Fiat Lux
with a length of flex,
its shift, its crick has made me
blink like a lemur at the lack
of the moon or a star
or a thing between. But it's good
how someone takes off their earrings
with the motion of shelling a pea.
A tiny snap. Like the hasp-click
of a calyx
at the press of a picker's thumb.
A sound like lifting an airtight lid
or a pin dropping in a pyramid.
Then the lobe's set free
and breathes with delight
to shed the slight weight
of the earrings.
Earrings that might be
twin filaments, a pair of ball-bearings
or a hammock-faced moon and a tarnished star.

Aphrodisiacs

The lengths I'd have gone to to lead you down
the Donegal cliffs to that grass-covered ledge
– the width of us – above the Atlantic.
No one would have seen us but apparently
that wasn't the point – the point was
it was over between us and you couldn't
pretend. That night, though, in the rented bed,
for peace of mind or for old times' sake,
you must have thought, Why not. Why not indeed.
For a start because it seems you'd catch
something I caught from someone by mistake
– suddenly at sea on her wine-coloured carpet
after eating several Chinese sweets
made from fine-textured black-bean paste.

Gulf

Two funerals in the one day were too much
to meet with without feeling life had some such
designs on us – both proceeding at the same pace
to within a stone's throw of the same place.
The women they passed all crossed their hearts
with a sign to divide them into quarters
while the men touched their crotches to avert
whatever it was made the dead inert.

A priest who flicked a palm frond led the first
up through the village to the place of rest:
Dives, the caterer, in a black, gilded hearse
drawn by a dazzling scarab of a horse
horned with black-azure plumes. Then came Lazarus
carried past on the fishermen's shoulders
down to the shore where his weight was lowered
for the sea to lay its cold hand on the wood.

Legacies

It was in the cellar of the Edinburgh house
owned by my great great grandfather

that the bodysnatchers, Burke & Hare,
unknown to him, kept their cache of corpses

in cold storage before delivering them
to the School of Human Anatomy.

There was always a skeleton in the closet,
or a skull at least, perched among the army berets,

the Luger, the greatcoat, the Zeiss binoculars
and the fox stole with its red glass eyes

and blackened lips which fastened with a snap.
There was always the skull in the clothes cupboard

with a fidgety script on its fontanel,
saying nothing, its eyes reduced to zeroes.

*

In today's newspaper I read of a Xhosa chief
who believed his great great uncle's skull was kept

somewhere in Scotland. After leaving several
military museums empty-handed,

he had a dream of a field and a white horse
grazing. In the field a barn, in the barn

that skull. And there it seems he found it
– on a shelf among some tarnished bridles –

identified by a bullet hole in the temple
from a British rifle. So some day soon

may we now expect a visit from a man
with or without a leopardskin and flywhisk

who has travelled across two continents to ask
what we've kept all this time in our closet?

Zeroes

As cunning as the steel-shod flea from Tula,
my wristwatch has a web drawn on its dial
—each hour is equal to one radial
while a black spider with a juddery pulse patrols
the web's circumference, always too late
to meet the shadow it hovers over
but consuming each second with a sated quiver.

Out beyond Earth's atmosphere, on Skylab,
for weeks they observed how several orb-web
spiders would cope with zero gravity.
Not well at first: their webs sheer gobbledygook.
They had to learn their weight meant nothing
by Bruce-like trial and error until
at last their webs were perfectly symmetrical

unlike on Earth where perfect webs would crash
without extra buttressing below.
But there, in the absence of flies, they fashioned
their nets into a heaven of pure ornament
and waited patiently for their reward.
—A flaw in the design lets the spirit escape,
as Spider woman taught the Navajo.

I never find that small trapdoor in time.
Here on my wrist the spider time draws in
the toughest substance of the natural world
and morning noon and night till zero hour
keeps casting her silk out over nothingness.
She quivers on a canny perspex disc
and flies without wings into inner space.

Galatea and Polyphemus
after Ovid

I think of the sheer foulness of Polyphemus
and then of the face of Acis which seems
unfair, it's so flawless. I lay all day
in his arms on a high green sheltered ledge
hidden from the Cyclops, that one horrid eye
molten with inflammation and fixated
on my image. I hate to think of my image
pinned down in each of his pitifully few
brain cells like a doll madonna stuck
in some wall shrine lit by a grey-pink bulb
on an alley of rats and gore and filth.
His outside's bad enough – hard ulcerated
slime a loathsome cindery mauve, his one eye
like an anus, a blob, a fronded jellyfish.
Then we heard him coming and watched him squat
on a jagged promontory, the waves matting
the pelt on his calves. He sets down that stick
tall as a ship's mast and starts puffing
at a pipe of giant reeds like a church organ.
I remember his song which went like this:

O Galatea tiny-featured as a chaffinch,
supple and slender as a rowan sapling,
smooth as Greek yogurt, as jasper beads,
silkier than the inside of an oyster
– like a secret tree in the middle of the wood
casting a violet shadow. Your breasts are
like new-made planets in the night sky
which make the stars drop from the firmament
to cluster round your feet like leaves on fire

–you fit so exactly into your skin
your small chiselled joints must be transparent...

I'll spare you some salacious details
of how he spied me bathing naked
–my breasts like bells of flesh, my nipples
parting the water ... his voice all thick and hectic
though bits of his song weren't actually so bad.
That's why I remember it. I wouldn't mind
Acis pirating a few of those lines
but he more than makes up for that lack
with the lines of his profile – even his wrists,
even his callussed heels are aphrodisiac
though his phrasing leaves something to be desired.
Cyclops then roughened his song with a lot of reproaches:

But, O Galatea, you're harder-hearted than gnarled oak,
falser than water, more slippery than ice,
vainer than peacocks and colder than the winter sea.
Worst of all and what I hate the most are
your sudden turns of speed in spurning me.
I'd bask in your other faults if I could just
once grab hold of you. Then see if you'd escape.
And think of all the things you're missing by not
being mine: all this mountainside, that plain
as far as those squalid dinky coast resorts
that spoil the view – I'll paste them with a layer
of mud and ash as soon as I feel myself again.
Think of the orchards bowed down with pears,
pale grapes and also black ones; my caves
uncannily tuned to body heat no matter
what season's abroad, dog days or Arctic blasts;
woodland fruits beside freshwater streams,
clumps of white-domed mushrooms, tall forests

of chestnuts, flocks of goats whose udders drip
with finest milk from which I make
clean curds by adding rennet. Are you mad?
Can't you see what I'm offering? I won't dull
your eyes with presents from the cornershop,
chocolates and daffodils – no diamanté jewels
like that cheapskate Acis gets to pin on you.
I'd dig rare gems out of the mountainside
with strange faults of fire like constellations
and fashion a necklace of dragonflies
and teach two tame owls to sing for you;
I'd twist curious lamps out of raw iron
to light you down the corridors of cave
to a bed of hoopoe crests where you would wait
for me to appear, my face dark with desire . . .
but you hate my face – it makes you cringe away.
So who says I'm that gruesome? I saw myself
in a blue pool today and thought – just look
at the size of him will you? Even Jove
who doesn't exist could never be bigger.
Does being hairy have to mean I'm vile?
Would you want a bald hound or horse, or a bird
without feathers? And if it's my one eye,
my uncompanioned eye, that bugs you what about
the sun? Two of them up there and we'd be flayed.
My eye grows on a single stem and follows
only you with its one shaft of devotion.
As for the muck on me, the stink, I'll scrub
myself with pumice every night before
we touch. Every night to touch you! O
Galatea, drop that skinny runt of an Acis
or let me at him and I'll tear his limbs
off his hairless trunk and fry them in Etna

whose channels of sulphur and blue fire
are coursing through my veins for love of you.
A love that scalds me and stops me working.
Take a look at my neglected flock. Entire fleets
pass by unscathed as if I were a lighthouse.
I just forget to wreck them. My whole life
is in arrears, in ruins like a great city
turned to burnt earth and swamps and column stumps
while all you do is quiver with disgust
at my offers and take to your exquisite heels
before I can quieten down my heartbeat
enough to speak let alone find the right words,
soft words, to let me creep closer . . .
                                    Raucous
and needled by his own song, he stood up
and happened to spy us – the tongue of Acis
making waves through me without the use of words
when the rocks trembled with the Cyclops's cry
'That's the last you'll ever taste of love.'
I dived in the bay but my poor Acis
still crouched in a daze, he couldn't move as
Cyclops hefted up a rock and hurled it
crushing him, its edge alone sufficient
to flatten him. Blood trickled out from under
like autumn streams dyed coppery with leaf-juice
and the dense mass of rock, as though through guilt,
cracked open and a tall green reed sprang up
and waters gushed through the hollow rock
and a new youth waded out mid-stream,
his temples crowned in a wreath of rushes,
the waters round him whispering his name.